Discovering Science

Power Station Sun

The story of energy

John Mason

Facts On File Publications
New York, New York • Oxford, England

Contents

NOTE TO THE READER: while you are reading this book you will notice that certain words appear in **bold type**. This is to indicate a word listed in the Glossary on page 45. This glossary gives brief explanations of words which may be new to you.

Photographic credits

t = top   b = bottom   l = left   r = right   c = center

5, 12 John Mason; 15l, 15r ZEFA; 21 Jonathan Scott/Seaphot; 25 ZEFA; 27 David Maitland/Seaphot; 29 ZEFA; 30 David Redfern Photo Library; 33 Flip Schulke/Seaphot; 34 ZEFA; 34/35 Oceaneering/Seaphot; 38/39 ZEFA; 40t Quadrant Picture Library; 40b Chris Howes/Seaphot; 41 National Coal Board; 42 ZEFA; 44 Chris Fairclough

Illustrations by Paul Doherty, Keith Duran/Linden Artists, Sallie Alane Reason, Chris Rothero/Linden Artists

Discovering Science/Power Station Sun

Copyright © BLA Publishing Limited 1987

First published in the United States of America by Facts on File, Inc. 460 Park Avenue South, New York, New York 10016.

All rights reserved. No part of this book may be reproduced or utilized in any form or by any means, electronic or mechanical, including photocopying, recording or by any information storage and retrieval systems, without permission in writing from the Publisher.

Library of Congress Catalog Card Number:
  87-80097

Designed and produced by BLA Publishing Limited, East Grinstead, Sussex, England.

A member of the **Ling Kee Group**
LONDON · HONG KONG · TAIPEI · SINGAPORE · NEW YORK

Printed in Italy by New Interlitho

10 9 8 7 6 5 4 3 2 1

The Sun and energy

Each day, the Sun rises in the morning and sets in the evening. Without it, we could not exist and the Earth on which we live would not have been formed.

If you look up into the sky on a clear, dark night you can see hundreds of stars. Our sun is also a star. Some stars are thousands of times more powerful than the Sun. They look like specks of light because they are so much further away than the Sun. The Sun is the nearest star to us. It is only 150 million kilometres (93 million miles) from Earth.

The Sun's energy

The Sun is very hot. Its surface has a **temperature** of 6000°C (11,000°F). You can feel the Sun's heat on your skin on a sunny day. All around you is the light of the Sun's rays. The heat and light of the Sun show us that it is giving out **energy** all the time. All living things need energy. You need energy to work, to run or even to breathe. Plants use the energy in sunlight to grow. Animals cannot do this.

▼ This picture of the Sun was taken from a spacecraft, using a special camera.

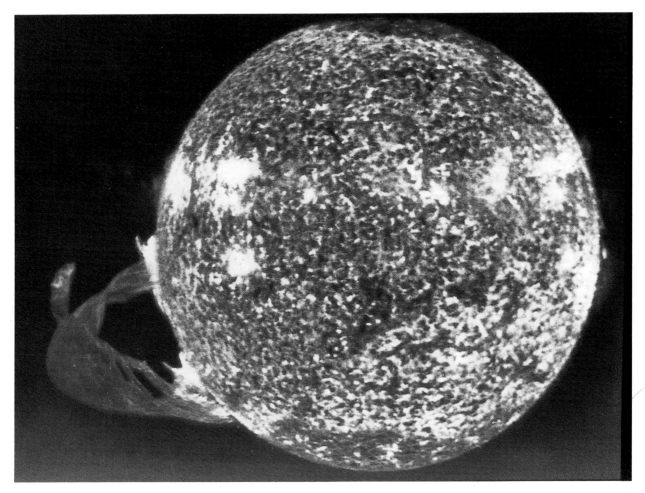

Day and night

The Earth is our home in space. It is part of a large family which contains one star (the Sun), nine **planets** and many other smaller bodies. The Earth is one of the nine planets. These all move around the Sun along paths called **orbits**.

The Sun is like a huge ball. It is more than one million times bigger than our Earth. The Sun gives out heat and light all the time. The planets shine only because they **reflect** the Sun's light.

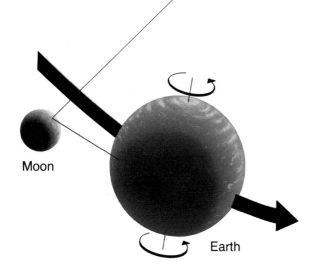

Sun

Moon

Earth

◄ Sun, Earth and Moon are all nearly spheres in shape. The way they move gives us our days, nights, months, seasons and years.

Like the planets, the Moon has no light of its own. By reflecting the light of the Sun, the Moon shines at night. We depend upon the Sun for our moonlight.

The spinning spheres

The Earth, Sun and Moon are all nearly **spheres** in shape, like oranges. They are spinning all the time. The Sun spins rather slowly. The Earth also turns as it moves around the Sun. It spins round completely once every 24 hours.

As the Earth turns, the Sun seems to rise in the east, move across the sky, and set in the west. After sunrise it is daytime. After sunset it gets dark.

Months and years

The Moon is the Earth's closest neighbor. It takes the Moon 27⅓ days to go once around the Earth. This period of time is called a **lunar month**.

The Earth takes 365¼ days to travel once around the Sun. This period of time is our year. There are thirteen lunar months in one year, but our calendar has only twelve months. Each of the calendar months is slightly longer than a lunar month.

The seasons

The Earth spins around an imaginary line which passes through its center. This is called its **axis**. The Earth's axis is tilted, and this tilt causes the seasons — spring, summer, fall, and winter.

In the winter, the Sun is low in the sky. The heat of the Sun is spread out more thinly than it is in the summer. Then the Sun climbs higher in the sky. This makes the land and the seas warmer in the summer and cooler in the winter.

Clocks and calendars are just our way of measuring the time it takes for all these things to happen.

▼ Earth takes one year to travel around the Sun. The longest day is in June and the shortest is in December.

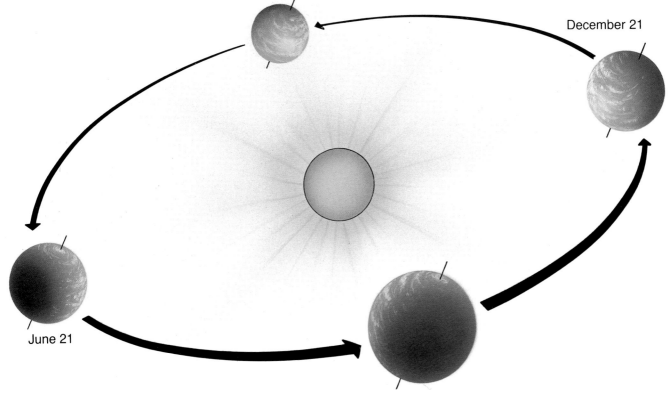

December 21

June 21

Looking at the Moon

Any object in orbit around the Earth is called a **satellite**. There are several thousand man-made satellites moving around the Earth. There is only one natural satellite. Its distance from the Earth is about 380,000 km (235,000 miles). The Moon is a small world. It would take 81 Moons to weigh as much as the Earth.

The surface of the Moon

The Moon is a strange place. It has no air. It also has no water. Because of this, plants and animals cannot grow or live on the Moon.

If you use binoculars or a small telescope you can see dark patches on the surface of the Moon. These are called 'seas', but there has never been any water in them. There are also huge mountain ranges on the Moon. The tallest of these are higher than Mount Everest. In places, deep valleys make their way across the Moon's surface.

The Moon is covered with circular areas called **craters**. They look like shallow saucers in the surface. In some places the craters overlap one another. Some craters are as much as 295 km (183 miles) across. Others are just tiny holes. The large craters have outer walls which are not very steep. Most scientists think that the craters were caused by **meteorites** hitting the Moon's surface.

The Moon's changing face

The Moon has no light of its own. Because of this, it shows changes of shape called **phases**. The Sun lights up only half of the Moon at a time. When the Moon is almost between the Sun and the Earth its dark side is turned towards us. Then we cannot see it shining. This is called new moon.

As the Moon moves along its orbit, a little of the sunlit side begins to show. First we see a thin **crescent**, then a half moon and then full moon. At full moon, the whole sunlit side faces us. After full, the Moon slowly becomes a half and then a crescent. Then it reaches new moon once again.

The Moon takes 27⅓ days to go once around the Earth. This is the same time the Moon takes to spin once on its axis. Because of this we always see only one side of the Moon. You can prove this by a simple experiment. Place any round object on the center of a table. This is your Earth. Choose another round object to represent the Moon. Move your Moon, without spinning it, slowly around your Earth. By the time your Moon has moved once around the Earth, both sides have faced the Earth. Now repeat the experiment, but keep one side of the Moon facing the Earth, all the way round. To do this, the Moon has to spin round once!

▼ In this picture, A is new moon, B and H are crescent moons, C and G are half moons. D and F are called gibbous moons, and E is full moon.

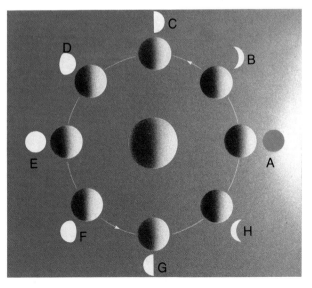

The Sun's family

The first **astronomers** saw that some star-like bodies seemed to move among the other stars in the sky. They called these 'wandering stars' or planets. A planet is not hot like a star is. It shines because it reflects the light of the Sun. The Earth, seen from space, shines like all the other planets.

The nine planets

Nearest the Sun are four small planets. These are Mercury, Venus, Earth and Mars. The Earth lies third in order of distance from the Sun.

Beyond Mars there is a wide gap. In that gap, there are thousands of rocky bodies called **asteroids**. Then come four giant planets. These are Jupiter, Saturn, Uranus and Neptune. The most distant planet is smaller than our Moon. It is called Pluto.

Mercury and Venus are closer to the Sun than we are. They show phases like the Moon. Mercury is a bit larger than our Moon. Like the Moon, it has craters and a rough surface. Venus has thick clouds of poisonous gas around it. On the surface it is very hot. No one could survive there.

Mars is also called the 'Red Planet'. It is further from the Sun than we are. It has very little air. Mars has ice caps at its poles, and many craters on its surface. No life has been found there.

Jupiter, Saturn, Uranus and Neptune are much further away. They have surfaces made of gas. Jupiter is a huge world. The Earth could fit inside it 1300 times. Saturn is smaller than Jupiter. It has a fine set of rings around it. It also has more than 20 of its own moons.

▼ The nine planets in the Sun's family. Mercury is the closest to the Sun and Pluto is furthest away.

Mars

Earth

Venus

Mercury

Jupiter

Sun

Uranus and Neptune are both smaller than Saturn. Uranus has a number of narrow rings.

The orbits of the planets

Mercury, the nearest planet to the Sun, takes only 88 days to go once round the Sun. Pluto, the furthest away, takes 248 of our years to complete its orbit. Pluto is most of the time further away than Neptune. However, it moves closer to the Sun than Neptune between 1979 and 1999. Its path is tilted. The other planets all orbit on much the same plane or level. It is known as the plane of the orbits.

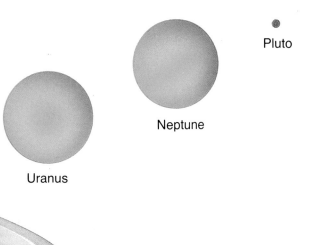

Pluto

Neptune

Uranus

Saturn

▼ The planets furthest from the Sun take the longest time to complete one orbit.

The other stars

If you flew round the world you would travel about 40,000 km (25,000 miles). In space, a distance like this is very small. The Sun, our nearest star, is 150 million km from us. The next nearest star to the Sun is 40 million million km away. This is one billion times the distance around the Earth!

The number of the stars

Look up at the sky on a clear, dark night. You can see hundreds of stars. Our star, the Sun, is just one of these. It belongs to a huge cloud of stars called the Milky Way **galaxy**. There are 100 000 million stars in this galaxy. Sometimes you can see the Milky Way as a glowing band of light stretching across the night sky.

The Milky Way is shaped like two fried eggs laid back to back. Our Sun is not at the centre. It is well out towards one edge. Our galaxy is not the only one. Telescopes can show millions of other galaxies. A few can even be seen without using a telescope.

▼ Galaxies contain millions of stars. This galaxy was photographed using a very large telescope.

▲ A picture by an artist showing our galaxy (the Milky Way) as it would be seen from the side. The position of the Sun and our planets is marked X. Our galaxy is just one of millions of galaxies.

▼ This picture shows some giant stars compared with the Sun. The Sun is the small white dot at the bottom right. Betelgeuse is 1200 times as bright as the Sun.

The size of the stars

Look at a star through a telescope. You will only see a tiny dot of light. This is because the stars are so far away. The Sun is much closer than all the other stars. You must NEVER look at the Sun through a telescope. It could blind you.

The Sun appears large and very hot to us. However, compared to other stars it is really quite small. Some of the stars we see in the night sky are much bigger than the Sun. They are also much hotter.

The Earth is covered with a blanket of air. As you go higher, the air gets thinner. There is no air at all when you reach empty space. In the vast spaces between the stars and planets there is no air of any kind. We call this a **vacuum**, which means empty. Most of the universe in which we live is nothing but empty space.

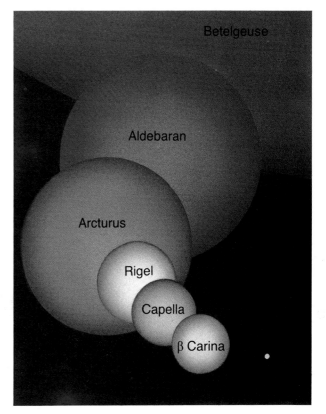

Betelgeuse

Aldebaran

Arcturus

Rigel

Capella

β Carina

What are things made of?

We live in a universe of great variety. All the things in the universe are made up of tiny pieces of **matter**. We use this word to describe anything that takes up space. All things on Earth are made of matter. Trees, houses, the land, the sea and the clouds in the sky are all made of matter. Your body, and even the air you breathe, is made up of matter.

Matter exists either as solids, liquids or gases. We call these the three states of matter. We can change matter from one state to another. We do this by heating it up or by cooling it down.

Think of water. It can be found in each of these three states. The ice in your refrigerator is a solid. The water that you drink is a liquid. Water turns to steam when it boils. Steam is a gas. The space taken up by any kind of matter is called its **volume**.

Solid matter

A solid will keep its shape. It always takes up the same volume. A pencil, a brick or a piece of wood does not change shape by itself. Also, it does not change the amount of space it takes up. We can make things out of solids. We can change their shape. Then they will stay as we have changed them. A piece of wood can be cut and shaped as we want it. So can a piece of metal even if it is very hard, like iron.

Gases

When a liquid is heated enough it changes to a gas. Water becomes steam at its boiling point of 100°C (212°F). Gases, many of which we cannot see, have no shape. They will spread out to fill as much space as they can find.

When air is heated, it expands to take up more room. Like any other gas it can be made to fill a container, such as a hot air balloon. If a balloon filled with air is burst, the air soon leaks away.

▼ When water freezes it becomes a solid, like the lumps of ice in this picture. The ice keeps its shape until it melts.

Liquids

Liquids, like solids, take up a certain amount of space. The milk in a bottle takes up a volume. If you pour it into a saucepan, it takes the shape of the pan. A liquid does not have a shape of its own like a solid. We cannot make things out of liquids. They will not keep their shape. When a solid is heated enough, it changes into a liquid. All metals have melting points. A piece of aluminum will melt and become liquid when it is heated to 660°C (1220°F).

What are atoms?

In ancient Greece there was a scientist called Democritus. He wondered what would happen if you kept on cutting a piece of matter into smaller and smaller pieces. He said that you would have a piece so small that it could not be cut any more. He called this piece of matter *atomos*, which means 'cannot be cut'. No one could prove if he was right or wrong.

We know that all matter is made of things called **atoms**. They are very small. Pick up a handful of fine sand. Try to pick out just one grain of sand. Atoms are even smaller. One grain of sand would have millions of atoms in it!

Smaller still

It is hard to imagine how small one atom is. To get some idea, look at one hair from your head. You could fit more than 150,000 atoms side by side in the width of this one hair.

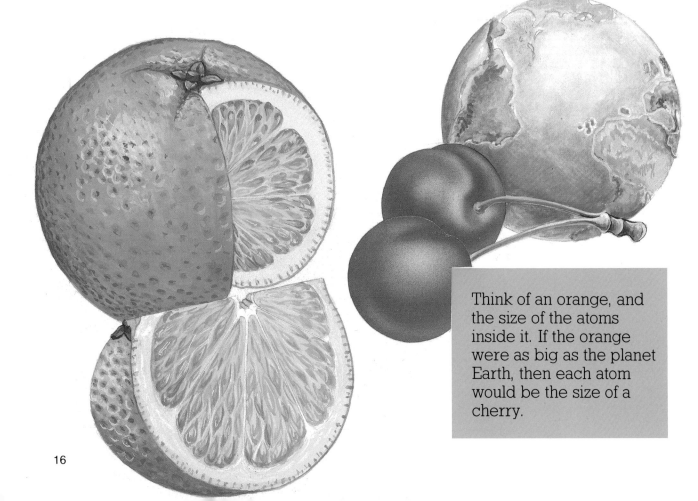

Think of an orange, and the size of the atoms inside it. If the orange were as big as the planet Earth, then each atom would be the size of a cherry.

Different kinds of atom

The atoms which make up the Universe are not all the same. There are 94 different sorts of atoms to be found. These are known as the **elements**. Each of these is different.

Elements often join in groups called **molecules**. They team up to make different kinds of matter. The 94 elements can join up in all sorts of ways. It is because of this that there are so many kinds of matter.

Think of all the words you would find in a large dictionary. These are all made up of just 26 letters. But there are 94 elements. It is no wonder that there are over four million different sorts of molecule in the universe.

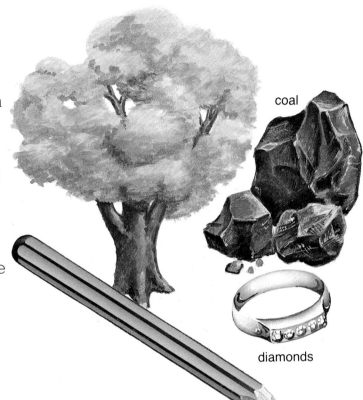

coal

diamonds

▲ Carbon is found in all living things. Coal, diamonds and graphite are all forms of carbon.

graphite

Carbon

The element carbon is very important. Although it is just one of 94 elements, we find it in many things we see around us. It occurs in all living things, in plants, in animals and in our bodies. The food we eat and the fuel we burn contain carbon.

It is the only element that can join up to form chains and rings. Each time a new atom is added to a chain, a new kind of matter is formed. There are thousands of different molecules with carbon in them. Carbon is like the letter 'a' or the letter 'e' in the alphabet. It is used over and over again.

Hot and cold

Water plays a large part in our daily lives. We drink it, we cook with it, we use it for washing. Like most other things, water is made up of millions of molecules. Each one contains two atoms of hydrogen, and one of oxygen. Most of the time, the water we use is in its liquid state. If we boil it, it gives off steam and becomes a gas. When we freeze water, it becomes a solid.

Vibrating molecules

What happens inside water when these changes take place? No one can see the molecules in water, but we know one thing about them. They are never still. They are trembling or **vibrating** all the time.

Look at the pictures. One is of boiling water, one is of cold water and one is of ice cubes.

The ice cubes are solids. The molecules in solids are fixed to each other, but they are not quite still. They vibrate as though they are held in place by springs.

▼ When water freezes it becomes a solid, like the lumps of ice in this picture. The ice keeps its shape until it melts.

When you take the ice cubes out of the freezer, they soon melt. They take up the heat of the room and become the liquid, water. The same molecules vibrate more, and move further.

If we now put water in a saucepan and heat it, the water will soon boil. This is when the molecules move around even more. They move faster and faster. In time, they break free from each other to form a gas. The water turns into a vapour. It evaporates. In gases, the molecules dart about at great speed.

Measuring temperature

The word temperature is used to show how hot or cold something is. It tells you how much the molecules are vibrating or moving. You use a **thermometer** to measure how hot or cold something is. This shows temperature on a scale of numbers. These are called **degrees**.

The Centigrade scale is easy to use. Water turns to ice at 0°C (32°F). This is known as its freezing point. It boils at 100°C (212°F). This is known as its boiling point.

When people are well, they have a normal temperature of about 37°C (98.6°F). When they are ill, this may rise. They may have to stay in bed until their temperature has returned to normal.

- The temperature in outer space is −270°C (−518°F).
- At the South Pole it can be as cold as −80°C (−176°F).
- Water freezes at 0°C (32°F).
- Butter melts at 31°C (88°F).
- Our normal body temperature is 37°C (98.4°F).
- The body temperature of a camel reaches 41°C (106°F).
- The temperature of the hottest desert reaches 58°C (136°F).
- Water boils at 100°C (212°F).
- Lead melts at 328°C (622°F).
- Iron melts at 1536°C (2797°F).
- Gold melts at 2900°C (5252°F).
- The surface of the Sun is 5800°C (10,472°F).

How light behaves

Light given off by the Sun travels through space in all directions. The Sun is our main **light source**. It gives us most of the light we need during daytime. At night, and on dull days, we use electric lights to give us extra light.

We cannot see light as it travels. We can only see things when light shines on them. This shows us how light behaves.

Look around you for shadows. You can make a shadow by holding your hand over this page. A shadow is an area that light from one source cannot reach. Stand a pencil on the page and see how many shadows there are. The darkest shadow will come from the strongest light source. Shadows tell us that light travels in straight lines.

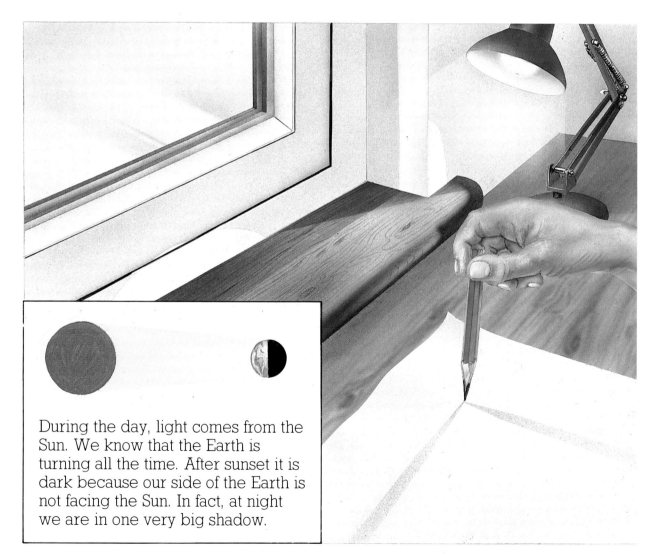

During the day, light comes from the Sun. We know that the Earth is turning all the time. After sunset it is dark because our side of the Earth is not facing the Sun. In fact, at night we are in one very big shadow.

Shade and shadows

On a cloudy day, there is still daylight, but the shadows are not so sharp at the edges. Sometimes you can hardly see any shadows at all. This is because the sunlight has to pass through the clouds.

Clouds are made up of millions of tiny drops of water. As the light goes through the clouds, it bounces off all the drops. We call this the scattering of sunlight. When light scatters it comes from many light sources at once. If there is a break in the clouds, the Sun shines through and we see dark shadows again.

▼ Water has a shining surface. It acts as a good reflector of light, as you can see in this picture.

cloudy day

sunny day

Reflections

When light strikes any surface it bounces back, just like a ball bouncing off a wall. This bouncing of light is called **reflection**. Light reflects very well off some things. A mirror is a good reflector. So is a piece of shiny metal, or an area of still water. Surfaces that are rough, or dark in color do not reflect light so well.

When we look into a mirror we see ourselves reflected very clearly in it. This is called our reflection. The surface of a mirror reflects nearly all of the light which falls upon it.

21

Can light bend?

One of the best ways to reflect light is by using a mirror. This is a piece of clear glass with a very thin layer of shiny metal on one surface.

Light travels in straight lines. It can only go around corners if we use something like a mirror to make it change direction. Shine a flashlight at a mirror held by a friend. If your friend moves the mirror around, the light from the flashlight will change direction.

Things we can see through

Some materials such as glass or clear plastic let light pass through them. Look around your home. You will find plenty of things you can see through. These things are called **transparent**.

With transparent materials, a little light is reflected from the surface, but most of it passes through. Look out of a window. You can see through it easily. Rays of light reflect from objects outside and

Bending light

You often see reflections of light. You can also show that light can sometimes bend. Fill a glass with water. Now place a drinking straw at an angle in the water. Place it so that the bottom half is under the water and the top half above the water. You will see that the straw seems to be bent. It appears to be bent at the place where it enters the water.

The straw is, of course, still quite straight. It only appears to bend. This bending of light is called **refraction**. The straw seems bent because the light changes direction slightly. It does this when it passes from air into water.

pass through the glass to your eyes. The rays are all bent slightly as they pass from the air to the glass. They all bend the same way so you do not notice it.

Frosted glass is sometimes used in houses. It lets light in but people cannot see through it. This is because the rays of light pass through the glass, but are scattered in many directions. Materials like this are called **translucent**.

Some materials do not allow light to pass through them at all. They are called **opaque**. When an opaque object is placed in a beam of light, it casts a shadow. The light cannot pass through it.

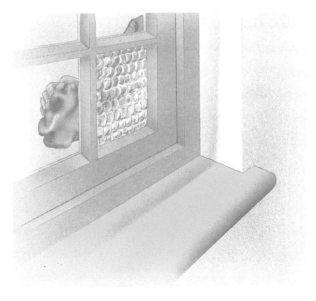

Can light be split?

Have you ever thought how dull the world would look if there were no colors? All the colors we see come from light.

A ray of pure light is without color. This pure light is called white light. Long ago, an English scientist called Isaac Newton discovered that white light contains a mixture of colored light. You can prove this for yourself by trying this experiment.

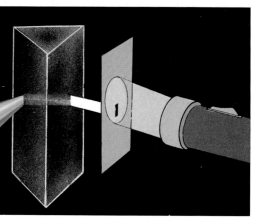

The colors of light
In a band of light there are seven different colors. We call these the colors of the **spectrum**. The colors are red, orange, yellow, green, blue, **indigo** and violet. Indigo is half way between blue and purple. It is named after the blue powder made from a plant.

You do not have to use a prism to see a spectrum. You can see one when you look at a rainbow. Here, the spectrum is made when light from the Sun is split by the raindrops. Each one of these acts like a tiny prism.

▲ When you next see a rainbow, name each of the colors one after the other. They will always be in the correct order of the colors of the spectrum.

The primary colors of light.

Primary colors

White light contains all the colors of the spectrum. It can also be made by mixing up just three. These three colors, red, green and blue, are known as the **primary** colors of light. When they are mixed, they make white light.

By mixing red and green light we get yellow. We only need to add the right amount of blue light to the yellow to make white light. We call blue and yellow **complementary** colors. We get white light by mixing them.

Yellow is a **secondary** color. It is made by mixing two primary colors, red and green. The other secondary colors are magenta (blue plus red), and cyan (blue plus green).

How color works

Colors in light are not the same thing as colors in paints. We know that white light can be split by a prism to give the colors of the spectrum. Now think of a paint box. It has a wide range of colors. These are not made by splitting white light.

You can only change white paint when you mix another color with it. White paint cannot be split up into other colors.

With paints, each color is made from one or more **pigments**. These are colored powders. They are made by grinding up different materials. Rocks, earths, plants and even dead insects are used. The colors in paints are not as pure as the colors in the spectrum.

What are tints?

We can make different strengths of any color when we are painting. These shades are called **tints**. We make tints by mixing the pure color. It can be mixed with white paint, or with a clear liquid such as water. This way, a skilful artist can use colors to bring out all the different tints seen with the eye. The artist can also use black paint to get different darker colors or shades.

How do we mix colors?

The three primary colors of light are red, green and blue. When we mix these we make white light.

The three primary colors of paint are red, blue and yellow. You can make most of the colors you need by mixing these three. Blue and red paints give you purple. Blue and yellow produce green. Red and yellow give you orange. When you mix red, green and blue in just the right amounts, you get black, not white.

Printing in color

The pictures in this book are printed with inks of just four colors. These are red (magenta), blue (cyan), yellow and black.

Look at this picture through a magnifying glass. You will be able to see thousands of small dots of color. You cannot see these with the naked eye. So you are not aware of them.

Where the dots of one color are close, the color looks dark or strong. You will see fewer dots of the color in the light areas. Tints in this book are not made by using white paint. The dots are spaced out to make light tints. Packed close, they make dark tints.

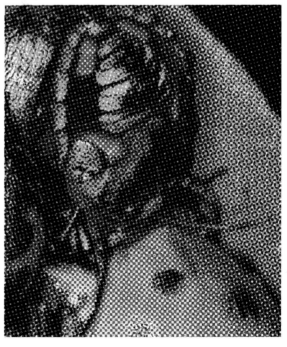

How we use colors

Colors are very important to us in our daily lives. Very often one color gives a message. We all know what it means. From an early age, colors help us to learn warning signs and signals.

Think of the color red. It often means 'danger', or 'warning', or 'take care'. Fire engines are painted red. They are easy to see when they are moving in traffic. Other cars soon get out of their way.

The fronts of trains are painted yellow. They may have black and yellow stripes. The color helps people to see a train coming from far away.

Colored lights are used where roads cross. Red, yellow and green traffic lights are used in most countries. Each of us knows that red means 'stop', and green means 'go'. Everyone must obey the traffic lights.

Colors for advertising

Color is used a lot in **advertising**. This is the name given to the way goods are brought to your notice. In towns, you often see bright posters or lights.

You feel you have to read the words. That way you may learn the name of a soft drink or a new car. It might even make you buy one. Advertising is done to persuade you to buy one kind of product instead of another.

Color is important in advertising. We soon recognize different goods by the colors used in the **advertisements**.

Often each firm will have its own color or design. You can soon spot the red cans of a well known soft drink, or the yellow and black on a film carton. You may have seen the blue and white paintwork of a Pan Am airliner.

Colors in sport

Color is used in all kinds of sport. Each team has its own colors. This means that the players can easily spot members of their own side. They can spot the other side too. Also the people watching can pick out the two teams at a distance.

Racehorse jockeys and racing cars have their own colors. People can spot the colors of the jockeys a long way away. Most racing cars look alike when speeding at 200 kph (125 mph) or more. It is the color of the car and the number that help you to pick out your favourite driver.

What are lasers?

Lasers are quite a new idea but most of us have heard of them. Many people just think of a laser as a way of making a beam of colored light in the sky. But laser light is very special.

A laser produces a very narrow beam of light. The beam does not seem to spread out. The light is of one pure color. Lasers have a great many uses, apart from light shows. They can drill, and cut hard metal. They are used for measuring distances. They can be used for sending and reading messages. Doctors in hospitals also sometimes use them in special operations.

Laser light
The laser makes a very narrow beam of colored light. It is very bright. The beam seems to go on and on. The light does not get any dimmer. Compare a laser beam to a car headlight. If you stand close to the headlight and look at it, it hurts your eyes. The further away from the car you go, the weaker the light becomes. It no longer hurts your eyes. The headlight beam spreads out. It gets wider and weaker.

The laser light beam is very thin. It takes very much longer to spread out. It is also far stronger than a car headlight.

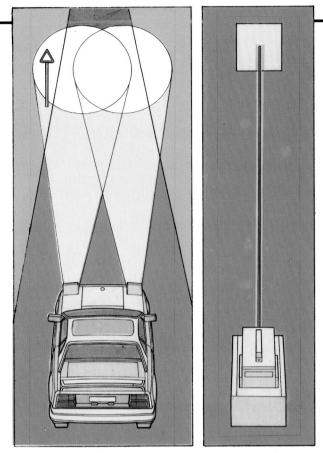

▲ A laser light beam is thin but very powerful. It does not spread out like other kinds of light.

How far to the Moon?

In 1969 the American Apollo astronauts left behind a special reflector on the surface of the Moon. Back on Earth, scientists pointed a powerful laser beam at the reflector on the Moon. They had to be very accurate. They used a telescope to fix its position.

Then a short burst of the laser beam was sent to the Moon. It reflected off the mirror straight back to the Earth. This took just over two and a half seconds. The scientists knew how long the laser light took, and how fast the light was travelling. So they could work out the distance between the Earth and the Moon. The Moon is about 380,000 km (235,600 mi) from us. Due to the laser beam, scientists were able to measure this distance to an accuracy of about 15 cm (6 in). This is less than the width of this page.

Keeping things cool

If you stay out in bright sunlight for too long, your skin will become burned by the heat of the Sun's rays. These rays enter the outer layers of the skin. Too much Sun may damage your skin. This causes sunburn. People with dark skins burn less easily. Their skin contains a dark substance which protects it. People with light skins burn quickly.

As the burnt skin heals, a dark color or suntan appears. This protects the skin against sunlight. Too much sunburn can make the skin very red and sore. Blisters may form and you may become ill.

Clothes in hot climates

In some parts of the world it is very hot and dry. Animals and humans must keep cool. The body must be **insulated** from the Sun's heat. People living in deserts or hot places such as India wear white, loose-fitting clothes and robes. The white color helps to reflect the light of the Sun away from the body. The loose fit means that air can flow freely under the clothes. This keeps the body cool. Some desert people still live in tents. These are open on one side to let the air pass through, keeping the inside of the tent cool.

Keeping cool in space

In space, there is no air to protect
astronauts from the fierce heat of the Sun.
The inside of a spacecraft must be kept
as cool as possible. Spacecraft have
white, shiny surfaces. These reflect most
of the heat from the Sun's rays. Inside a
spacecraft the temperature must be right
for astronauts to work in comfort.

Coming back to Earth

When a spacecraft comes back to
Earth from space it has to re-enter the
atmosphere. The spacecraft does this at
very great speed. It gets very hot as it
rubs against the air in the atmosphere.
The spacecraft has to be protected by a
heat shield. Without this, the spacecraft
and its crew would burn up.

Keeping things warm

▲ Eskimos wear fur-lined clothes to keep out the cold. This Eskimo's boots are made of sealskin.

▶ Deep-sea divers wear special suits to keep warm.

Few people have **adapted** to living in the cold, frozen wastes near the North and South Poles. In the Arctic, the Eskimos have learned how to protect themselves from the cold.

We all make heat in our bodies to keep the blood at the right temperature. To keep this heat in, Eskimos have learned to insulate themselves from the cold. They wear loose-fitting clothes which trap a layer of warm air inside. These clothes are made of thick fur to keep out the cold. They are also dark in color. Dark colors take in the heat. They do not reflect it away. Eskimos also rub fat over their skin. This layer of fat helps to keep out the cold.

Keeping body heat

Humans are **warm-blooded** animals. They produce heat within their bodies. This keeps the blood at a steady temperature. If this rises or falls by only a little, it can be very serious. People who work in very hot or cold places have to insulate themselves.

A deep-sea diver goes where it can be very cold. A diving-suit protects the diver against the cold water. A dry suit has a helmet with a small window in it. This is joined to a metal chest piece. The chest piece is fixed to a suit made of rubber and canvas. Air flows around the diver's body inside the suit. This helps protect the diver's body against the cold outside.

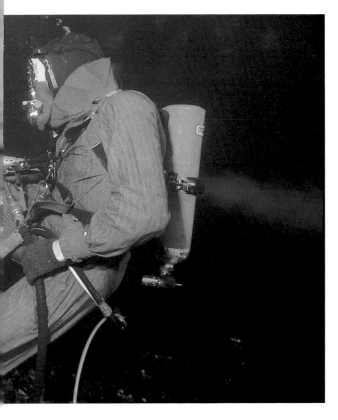

The greenhouse effect

Have you ever noticed how warm it is inside a car that has been standing in the sunshine? Sunlight passes through the glass windows and heat gets trapped inside the car.

Walk into a greenhouse. Even on a dull day, you soon realize how well it acts as a heat trap. The Sun sends out most of its heat in the form of light rays. These pass easily through the glass of the greenhouse.

The rays are then taken in by the plants and soil inside the greenhouse. The plants get warm. This raises the temperature inside the greenhouse. The warm soil and plants also give out heat, but not as rays of light. These new rays of heat cannot pass back through the glass. They are trapped inside the greenhouse. This raises the temperature inside. It is called the greenhouse effect.

All life on Earth depends on green plants. All plants need sunlight to grow. They change this light into other forms of energy. Animals can then use this energy.

35

Insulation and conduction

Heat is a form of energy. A fire gives out so much heat that you can feel it when you stand close by. Firefighters need to go into places where it is very hot. Their bodies must be protected from the flames and heat. They wear protective suits. The suit is a kind of heat barrier. It keeps out the heat of the fire, but it keeps in the normal heat of the body. A heat barrier is often called an **insulator**.

Vacuum flask

A thermos flask is another sort of heat barrier. It is a container with two glass walls. There is no air at all between the two walls. This is a vacuum. Another name for this type of flask is a vacuum flask.

A vacuum flask stops heat passing from inside the bottle to its surroundings. It also stops heat entering the bottle. It can be used for storing hot things, or cold things. Whatever is put inside the flask will keep its temperature.

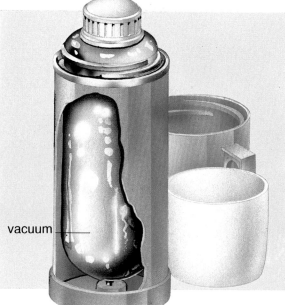

vacuum

Insulation and conduction

Conduction

Put a metal spoon in a cup of hot tea.
The handle of the spoon soon becomes
warm. Heat travels along the spoon by
conduction. Anything that lets heat pass
easily through it is a good conductor of
heat. Most metals are good conductors.

Wood is a very poor conductor.
A saucepan is made of metal, but the
handle is often made of wood. It can
be held when hot.

A stone floor feels cold to your bare
feet. A rug on the same stone floor feels
warm. Your feet are warmer than either,
so heat flows away from them.

The stone is a better conductor than
the rug. The stone takes the heat away
from your feet faster. So it feels cold. In
the same way, metals feel cold to the
touch. Wood and plastic do not.

Solar heating

Huge amounts of energy come from
the Sun. We can make use of this
energy by changing it into heat for our
homes. Some houses have a special
kind of box in their roof. This box,
called a solar panel, has a glass top
and a black plate inside. Water flows
through this plate. This water is
heated during the day by the Sun's
rays. When warmed, the water is
stored in an insulated tank for use
at night.

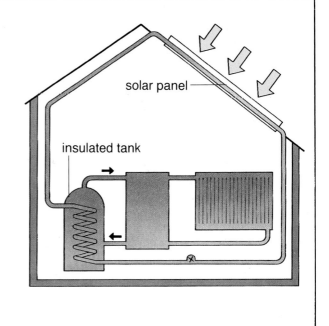

solar panel

insulated tank

Why does the world need energy?

All things need energy to make them work. A plane carrying a load of people a long way needs fuel for its engines. Cars, trucks, trains and ships all need fuel. They cannot work without it. People also need fuel to make their bodies work.

The world's cities need a huge amount of energy. Think of all the electricity which is needed. Streets, homes, shops, factories and offices all need heat, light and power. Much of this is made, or **generated**, by machines which use coal, oil and gas as fuels. Today, these fuels are being used up too fast.

Some countries use nuclear fuels to generate electricity. The atoms in these fuels are made to split. When this happens a huge amount of energy is released. This is called nuclear energy.

Fuel for our bodies

All of us need energy to do work. This comes from the food we eat. We use this as our 'fuel'. People all over the world need food to live, grow and work.

The poorer countries of the world cannot afford to buy all the food and fuel they need. As the number of people increases it becomes more and more difficult to grow enough food and to get enough fuel. The world's energy needs are now very great. Will supplies run out one day?

What are fossil fuels?

When an airliner takes off, the engines have to work very hard. They burn a large amount of fuel. The fuel used by planes and by cars, trains and ships, comes from oil.

The world depends very much on oil, coal and natural gas. These are known as **fossil fuels**. They are found beneath the Earth. They were formed there 300 million years ago.

What are fossils?

Fossils are the remains of living things. Long ago these took energy from the Sun. These living things died and fell to the ground. Over millions of years, sand and clay piled on top of these remains and their stored energy.

The weight from above pressed down on the material and packed it tight. Coal, oil and natural gas were all made in this way. They lay beneath the ground for millions of years. They stored the Sun's energy within them.

▼ This picture shows the fossil of a fish that lived millions of years ago.

▲ This is a modern coal-cutting 'shearer' in action.

What is coal?

Coal is made of the remains of giant ferns and trees which covered parts of the Earth long ago. These plants were made up of many elements including lots of carbon. The hardest coal is the best for burning. Most of it is pure carbon.

Mining coal

Most coal is found under the ground, so it has to be dug out. This is called coal mining. There are two sorts of coal mines. These are shaft mines and strip mines.

In shaft mines a hole is dug deep beneath the ground into the seam of coal. The coal can then be dug out. In strip mining, the coal is very near the surface. The miners use power shovels to clear away the soil and rocks that cover the coal. They can then dig it out.

What is oil?

Oil comes from the remains of living things. These lived in shallow seas millions of years ago. As they died and rotted, they were covered by layers of mud and sand. Their remains slowly turned into oil. The oil lies trapped under the ground. It is found by drilling down through the rock above it.

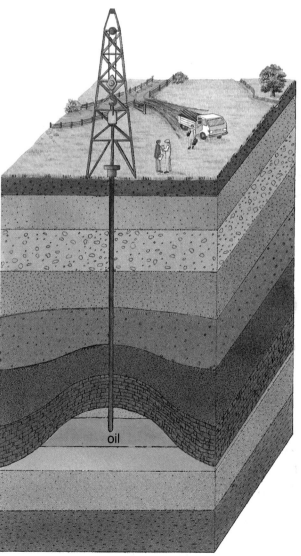

oil

Other forms of energy

The world gets most of the energy it needs from fossil fuels. In 100 years from now, coal may be the only fossil fuel left for us to use. All the oil and gas will probably be used up.

People will have to change the way they live and work. As oil gradually gets used up, we will need to find other kinds of energy. We call these **alternative energy** sources.

Solar energy

We know that huge amounts of energy come from the Sun. In the last 30 years, people have worked hard to find ways of getting power from the Sun. This is called **solar energy**.

Today, most countries in the world use some solar energy. This can be used for heating water and making electricity. Solar energy only works well when the Sun is shining. However, the heat from the Sun's rays can be stored for quite a long time. In some places, such as Sweden, houses are heated by solar energy all through the year.

Energy from water

We can also use the power of fast-flowing water. The water is led through a channel to a large wheel with blades.

▲ A hydroelectric dam in Pakistan.

The blades are made to turn by the water as it flows past. This makes the wheel turn, and this gives power. The wheel with its blades is called a **turbine**.

Turbines work very well. They turn very fast. They can be used to make electricity. This is known as **hydroelectric** power. Today, one-fifteenth of the energy used by the world is made this way.

Energy from the tides

The tides rise and fall twice each day. There is a lot of energy that could be used from this movement of the seas. It is not easy to find good places to build tidal power stations. They have to be near the mouths of large rivers. Here there is a strong flow of water all the time.

Think of the power and energy in waves. There must be some way of using this free power! But scientists say that it would be very hard to change this power into electricity and bring it ashore.

Power from the wind

Energy from the Sun heats up the air close to the Earth's surface. This makes the winds blow. So the energy that drives sailing boats comes in the first place from power station Sun.

Wind has been used as a source of power for thousands of years. Windmills were first used more than 500 years ago. They were used for grinding corn. They pumped water into fields so that the crops would grow.

Wind power was first used for making electricity in 1890. Today, some huge windmills are being built to do this. They are called wind turbines.

Wind turbines use blades instead of sails. The blades are very large. Some wind turbines have blades which are 50 meters (164 feet) long. The higher the speed of the wind, the more energy it contains. These wind turbines are put in places where there are high winds all the year round.

Wind power has two main advantages. The machines can be built quickly and cheaply. Also, the highest wind speeds are in the winter. This is when power is needed most.

▼ In the future, wind turbines like these may be seen on many windy hilltops.

Glossary

adapt: to change so as to suit changing surroundings and conditions

advertisement: a message giving people information about goods or services for sale. An advertisement may be printed, filmed or broadcast

advertising: drawing people's attention to goods or services for sale

alternative energy: another way of producing power that does not use fuels like oil, coal and gas. Power from sunlight, wind and waves are forms of alternative energy

asteroid: one of many thousands of small, rocky objects that revolve in orbits around the Sun

astronomer: a person who studies the Sun, Moon, planets, stars and galaxies

atom: the smallest part of any element that can exist having all the properties of that element. All the matter in the universe is made up of different atoms

axis: an imaginary straight line around which a body, such as the Earth, spins or seems to spin. You can imagine the Earth's axis as passing through the North Pole and South Pole

complementary: describes colors of light which make white light when mixed together

conduction: the movement of heat or electricity through an object

crater: a hollow in the ground shaped like a bowl. Many craters can be seen on the surface of the Moon

crescent: the curved shape of the Moon when it seems to form less than a half circle

degree: the unit used for measuring temperature. Water boils at 100 degrees centigrade (212 degrees Fahrenheit). This is written as 100°C (212°F)

element: a simple substance made of one type of atom. There are more than 90 elements in the universe

energy: the power to do work

fossil fuel: a material such as oil, coal or gas that is used to make heat or power by burning. Fossil fuels are formed from the remains of plants and small animals that lived millions of years ago

galaxy: a huge collection of stars, dust, planets and gases in outer space. The Sun, Earth and the other planets belong to a galaxy called the Milky Way

generate: to produce. Electricity is generated by a generator in a power station

hydroelectric: producing electricity from the energy in moving water

indigo: indigo is a bluish dye made from a plant of the pea family. Indigo is the name we use to describe the color that lies betwen blue and violet in the spectrum

insulate: to enclose or cover with a material so as to reduce the amount of heat passing in or out

insulator: any material through which heat or electricity will not pass

light source: an object from which light rays travel. The Sun, electric light bulbs and the flames from a fire are all light sources

lunar month: the time it takes for the Moon to travel around the Earth in its orbit. This is $27\frac{1}{3}$ days

matter: the material from which all things in the universe are made

meteorite: the remains of a small piece of matter from outer space called a meteor. Meteors burn up completely as they pass through the atmosphere. Larger meteors that do not burn up completely are called meteorites. They fall to Earth as lumps of hard rock or metal

molecule: the smallest amount of a substance that can exist on its own. Molecules usually consist of two or more atoms joined together

opaque: describes any substance that light cannot pass through

orbit: the path of a satellite as it circles around another object in space

phase: a gradual change throughout one month in the face of the Moon as seen from the Earth. The phases of the Moon are new moon, first quarter, full moon and third quarter

pigment: a substance, such as colored earth, that can be ground to a powder and used in paints

planet: a large body in space that revolves around the Sun. The Earth is a planet, so is Mars

primary: describes one of three colors which can be mixed to produce other colors. The primary colors of light are red, green and blue. Those of paint are red, yellow and blue

prism: a solid lump of glass or other transparent material that is used to bend rays of light

reflect: to turn back. When a mirror reflects a beam of light, it turns it back

reflection: what happens when a beam of light is turned back by a shiny surface. You see a reflection of your face when you look in a mirror

refraction: the bending of light

satellite: a body in orbit around another body in space. The Moon is a satellite of the Earth

secondary: describes a color that can be made by mixing two primary colors

solar energy: energy produced by using the rays of the Sun

spectrum: the rainbow of colors made when white light is split by a prism or by drops of water

sphere: a solid, round body such as a ball or a globe

temperature: the measure of how hot or cold something is. Temperature is measured in units called degrees

thermometer: an instrument used for measuring the temperature of something

tint: the strength of a color

translucent: describes any substance that some light can pass through. A sheet of white paper is translucent

transparent: describes any substance that lets light pass through easily. Clear glass and water are transparent

turbine: a shaft to which a number of curved blades are fixed. The turbine is made to turn at high speed by a gas or by a jet of water

vacuum: a space that contains no air

vibrate: to move to and fro, or up and down, quickly. If you beat a drum it vibrates

volume: the space taken up by something

warm-blooded: describes animals whose bodies stay the same temperature, whatever the temperature of the surroundings